Touchstones

poems by

Roberta Schultz

Finishing Line Press
Georgetown, Kentucky

Touchstones

*"The fool doth think he is wise, but the wise man
knows himself to be a fool."*
—Touchstone from Shakespeare's As You Like It

*"The true spirit of delight, the exaltation, the sense of being more than
Man, which is the touchstone of the highest excellence, is to be found in
mathematics as surely as poetry."*
—Bertrand Russell

*"But still, no matter how much time passes, no matter what takes place in
the interim, there are some things we can never assign to oblivion, memories
we can never rub away. They remain with us forever like a touchstone."*
—Haruki Murakami

Copyright © 2020 by Roberta Schultz
ISBN 978-1-64662-274-0 First Edition
All rights reserved under International and Pan-American Copyright Conventions.
No part of this book may be reproduced in any manner whatsoever without written permission from the publisher, except in the case of brief quotations embodied in critical articles and reviews.

ACKNOWLEDGMENTS

"At Somerset Place: Washington County, NC" was previously published in *The Main Street Rag*, Volume 22, No. 4 Fall 2017
"After the Polls Closed on Election Day," was previously published in *For a Better World*: 2018
"Complicit" appears in *Pine Mountain Sand & Gravel: Appalachia Acting Up*, Volume 21, 2018
"Song" appears in *Pine Mountain Sand & Gravel: Appalachia: Stay or Go?* Volume 20, 2017
"Tarzan at the Wiedemann's Picnic," appears in *Riparian*, Dos Madres Press, 2019
"What's Missing?" exhibited as a broadside in "50 Years of The Blue Ash Review," University of Cincinnati Blue Ash Gallery, September 26-October 11, 2019

Publisher: Leah Maines
Editor: Christen Kincaid
Cover Art: Karen L. George
Author Photo: Roberta Schultz
Cover Design: Elizabeth Maines McCleavy

Order online: www.finishinglinepress.com
also available on amazon.com

Author inquiries and mail orders:
Finishing Line Press
P. O. Box 1626
Georgetown, Kentucky 40324
U. S. A.

Table of Contents

Ode to Prayer 1

The Truth Is 2

Clip-ons 4

Complicit 6

After the Polls Closed on Election Day 7

The Meaning of My Father's Bundle 9

My Sister, the Stylist 10

That Creature Called Confidence 12

Secret Strength 13

On Hearing the Diagnosis 14

At Somerset Place, Washington County, NC 15

Dudley Walks the Red Carpet at the VA 16

Tarzan at the Wiedemann's Picnic 18

John Donne and God 19

Requiem 20

The Webster Sisters Discuss Theology 21

That Kind of Woman 23

Migration 24

Elegy for My Ancestry Kit 25

Rosaries 27

Touchstone 30

Song 31

The Bear Medicine 32

What's Missing 35

Ode to Prayer

Plainsong in ancient unison.
Chant in vocables.
Little grunt with stomps and dance.
Memorized ritual from ordained tongues.
One low growl sung in Sanskrit.

You do not cure cancer
or change final numbers
on a scoreboard.

Still, the point guard
kisses her medal.
The quarterback
takes a knee.

Fingers rub woven fabric
on tiny dolls, slide over beads
segmented like slick scarabs.

Do you remember
blood sacrifice?

Now you settle
for so little:

pilgrim rocks scattered
on the gravesite,
desperate petitions forged
in foxholes,
quiet tug at the dreamcatcher
slung casually from my
rearview mirror.

The Truth Is

As her head bows in morning ritual
she offers golden nourishment to Bast.
I conjure the humble curve of her spine.

Gauzy robes flutter with last act of supplication:
a spoon taps on blue and white chipped china
to loosen stubborn morsels, then clangs to the floor.

The Cat Goddess snakes over splayed ankles
with arched back. She spirits the fallen celebrant down river
on a wide royal barge loaded deep with honeyed beer.

Servant and master are cast together in likeness—
stamped on amulets worn by the bronzed men
who shoulder carved boxes to the western shore.

Her son the cop finds her face-down in the cat food
where blood pools near her right cheek.
Later, the undertaker scrapes his lumpy effigy,

shapeless and fish belly white. Botched work mocks
memory of her baby doll voice— that jingle
like charm bracelets dangled from a rearview mirror.

She read to us—her dazzled nieces—in magic incantation:
"Rapunzel, Rapunzel, let down your hair
that I might climb the golden stair."

Pouting lipstick, bright red, she was part Brigitte Bardot,
part Marilyn in bikinis and pearls that framed our dress-up days.
We plumped cups of her old strapless gowns with tissues,

strutted around, faces and nails painted to match
in wayward pinks and savage purples while she plunked
on a gray guitar, "Way down in Columbus, Georgia."

We say our goodbyes to a mangled stranger
packed into salmon-colored polyester,
Cat Goddess sacrificed to an animal shelter, unsung.

Each morning I invoke her ceremony:
measure out heartbeats in reverent teaspoons,
bend to feed the endless feline hunger.

Clip-ons

I. My mother told me that her Aunt Loretta was a loose woman.
She shared this as we sat on the front stoop
under the one remaining shade tree along 12th Street.

I don't recall the kind of tree.
Newport spoke a different language then
where "tree" sufficed most of the time
since trees were categorized good or bad
depending on what they did or didn't drop
into gutters and downspouts.

I do remember the smell of armpits in summer heat
which may or may not translate
into "Chinese Chestnut" in my new tongue.

I asked my mother what made Aunt Loretta "loose"
because I'd never heard anyone described that way
in my limited schoolyard lingo.

My mother planted a seed in the soil of my unwashed ears
where—presumably—potatoes would grow
if I didn't use the wash rag
like my Grandma Babe taught me.

My mother whispered into this fertile garden
that Aunt Loretta had pierced ears.
Her eyes widened to indicate that the next words
offered more scandal: "and ran around on Mt. Adams!"
She released this secret in a mist of sighs.
And so, I never pierced my ears.

II. My sister combs the bins at yard sales
to bring me costume jewelry from a time gone by—
Clusters of blossoms climb the trellis of my earlobe,
lion head door knockers guard the garden path.
large dangly globes sparkle and swing reflections
at the summer moon.

III. No one else heeds my mother's fable,
including my mother.

We bury her in cherished diamond studs.
My sisters flank the coffin in tasteful pearl posts,
the only grand daughter's ear completely bordered in silver,
her entire arm a tattooed masterpiece.

I alone stand sentry in the shade
where dual lions bare indignant teeth.

Complicit
*"That's when she slapped me. Left me holding my mouth
and stomach devoured by shame."* —Natalie Diaz

"She bleeds if you breathe on her." That's
what Mommy told Dr. Hoy when
Violet tracked blood through his office. She
bore the brand of handprint where someone slapped
her cheek. Clutching her nose, Violet shuffled toward me.
Her heart-flecked hanky bloomed red, left
a trail of droplets leading toward me.
I cowered, lowered my eyes, holding
Mommy's hand. All clues pointed toward my
guilt, my anger. My mouth
clamped tight, incisors locked on lower lip, and
I stared down at stained tiles. While my stomach
growled, I prepared to be devoured
by the lie of silence, by
shared knowledge of our shame.

After the Polls Closed on Election Day

my mother's back straightened.
No stooped shoulders or downcast
eyes. Her mouth drawn in a line
of defiance, she did not fawn or keen

while shuffling the bags of groceries
up the walk from the Volkswagen
to the salmon colored metal cabinets
that flanked our ranch house kitchen.

In practiced relay, my sisters
and I crouched to stuff
those low makeshift pantries
with bread, can goods, cereal packs,

instant teas and coffees
while my mother stashed
quart jugs of beer in the fridge
and fish sticks in the freezer.

One night—Saturday—
we were allowed to sip
soft drinks from straws.
But not on Tuesdays

when my father tripped
through the door at 7:30
already "three sheets,"
as Mommy called it, from his stop

at Shorty's. That Election Night
we drank Nestea from tall
plastic tumblers crammed
with ice cubes.

And while Daddy stumbled
to the living room, slurring
"bring your old daddy a beer,"
we set the table and giggled.

I peeled off from the assembly line
long enough to deliver a quart jug
of Hudepohl and a tiny glass
to the lounge chair where

Daddy slumped, his back to us all.
"In your heart, you know he's right,"
my father bellowed to no one in particular.
He downed a quick beer shot

then looked over his shoulder
and over his glasses at my mother,
who deliberately stirred a pot
of spaghetti sauce at the stove.

"That's one good thing about voting
booths, Bobby." My mother grinned
that smile that made you realize
too late you would be smacked

full on the head with a hairbrush.
"Nobody goes in there but you
and your conscience. And I will sleep
well tonight knowing that my vote

cancelled yours out."
Daddy said no more. He took
his supper in the living room where
he chewed slowly in his chair.

The Meaning of My Father's Bundle

I. *Then*: after the sweat lodge
   while we talk in circle
      MJ smiles, telling how

Ojibwa women carry
   sacred bundles for those
      who walk on.

She says, "I have carried
   my mother's bundle
      for a year." I imagine

small leather pouch
   adorned with strips
      of pony beads, a deer skin

bag stuffed with tobacco
   or feathers. I cannot see
      beneath her words.

II. *Now*: I walk with a stone
   in my shoe that rubs
      stubborn holes in my sock.

Uneasy, I tip-toe.
   "Walk on eggs," Mommy said.
      But nothing stops

the wearing tear of fabric
   as stone grinds down
      to gravel, unraveling

my shuffle. Trying not to crush
   remaining grains, I dance
      on shells of molecules.

My Sister, the Stylist

She combs my hair straight up
through fingertips, eyes the ragged ends
You've been twiddling again.
She scolds me with a laugh that accepts
my unevenness, recognizes my bent
toward inevitable asymmetry.

I am in the salon chair, pumped
to the level where my head rests
at her mid-chest, just below her reflection
in the mirror.
She begins to clip away evidence
of my nervous habit.

While she sculpts split and twisted wisps,
she also styles a defense for Uncle Billy,
her favorite topic these days after chemo,
after launched glass beads of radiation
target the scattered constellation of cancer
that dots her liver.

I don't think he needs defending,
but ask her, *what exactly did Uncle Billy do
to make you love him so much?*
She smiles, looks up toward the corner of the ceiling,
taps her chin with the rat-tailed comb.

He always treated me like gold.
Like I was important.

I watch her long, thin fingers move
with precision over the brushy landscape
of my scalp, finding their rhythm,
working the shears to master tangles
and lop-sided growth.

She smiles at my well-groomed condition,
however temporary, and presses the pink
hand mirror into my palm while she swivels
the salon chair so that I now face
the other customers.

Right now what I want most
is to hand her the mirror,
invite her to sit and look back
at her life's intricate braid—
how it folds us in, strand by strand,
over solid shoulders of wonder.

That Creature Called Confidence

She hides
in the tall grass
of my hair.

Peeks over scruffy
curls at a morning
wild with teeth.

Coyotes howl
from the gorge.
Foxes prowl
the lake.
Big cats growl
through the tense woods.
Their shrieks
hang in the fog.

How can she rise
when the skies teem
with eagle eyes
and hungry hawks?

Her spotted body tilts
on thin fawn legs
as she darts

into newfound balance,
bounds the impossible fence.

Secret Strength

Your ears grow bigger
with age is what
I've always heard.

That's bad news
for my sister who thinks
hers are huge.

I check mine daily
in the mirror for size,
but they just seem longer,

though I didn't pierce them,
or become a loose woman
like Aunt Loretta.

They are still flat against
my head, but grown,
unlike Rosanne's.

Hers try to cup forward
like someone
straining to hear.

She doesn't even
have to use her hand.
They just stick out on their own.

When we were kids,
Dumbo was a Disney cartoon
about secret strength.

Now it's a live-action
first run movie.
Look out, world.

We Webster sisters
are fixing to fly.

On Hearing the Diagnosis

The waiting is the hardest part,
Tom Petty wails from the speaker.
At times, his singing breaks my heart.

His voice cracks, unlike classic art
(with lute and vocals sleeker)
and yet he nails the hardest part.

Anticipating from the start,
my ear becomes the seeker
of raw bone tones that break my heart.

The doctor strains to read the chart,
then clears his throat, seems meeker,
now how to say the hardest part…

His words stab swiftly like darts—
no cure swirls from a beaker.
Stage four—shatters waiting hearts.

In silence now let us depart.
That song to me seems bleaker,
The waiting is the hardest part,
and now, all singing breaks my heart.

At Somerset Place, Washington County, NC

Sycamores tower
over the open wound
of a lanced swamp.
Canals carved by dark hands
still drain away rot.

Tourists read plaques
while careful interpreters
couch plantation history
in phrases like
the enslaved.

> Hands too small to dig
> played gourd shakers
> and wooden flutes
> at Miss Sookie's, learned
> the way to free time.

> Eyes too wide to look
> down or narrow focus
> searched high windows
> for that vast expanse
> of unchained blue.

Dudley Walks the Red Carpet at the VA

Dark faces approach him
single file from the far corridor
as he scoots along just past
the slow revolving door.

He speaks to one slack sadness,
takes notice how Don's eyes search the floor,
"How it be, Black Pharaoh?" Shoulders arch,
stiff gait glides into dance.

Don clutches Dudley's open hand
close to his chest to answer, "My brother!
We only let them live in our world,"
Don swaggers upright at last.

Next, a stealth stalker clings near walls
with sideways glances to scope each corner
for explosions or shadows.
Dudley—in his Michelin Man puffy coat,

his house shoe-like loafers
that ease diabetic swelling—greets Wayne
with "What's happening, my brother?
How it be?" The onyx sheen of Wayne's face shatters.

Light flickers inside thick amber
as eyes behold an open-armed angel
who welcomes all that falter. Wayne lingers
on the red carpet where sun spills gold.

Joanne and Esther end their long shift
in shared secrets.
Tight curls glint under neon,
white teeth flash easy grins.

"Good morning, my Black Queens!"
Dudley croons the long "e"
a serenade to sweep sore feet
over the hospital threshold.

The nurses know him, his bronze star,
his photo in the paper alongside
a stretch limo hearse, daily maneuvers
down this hallway toward recovery.

"Good morning, yourself, handsome!"
Esther plays along in his pageant,
clearly enjoys this ritual
of call and response.

The drum facilitator side-steps the carpet
to hurry past Dudley. His eyes widen
at the eventual sight of her pacing backwards
to face him. "Al-bert-a!"

He sings the question,
"What's happening?"
She chants in turn,
"Everything, now that you're here!"

His head rocks in explosive laugh.
"I'll be there soon," but his cadence
pounds steady while Alberta races
down the hallway to the auditorium:

"Black Queen! Black Pharaoh!
What's happening?
How it be?
How it be?"

Tarzan at the Wiedemann's Picnic

It was Tarzan's fault that I ended up
on the banks of the Ohio—
all that vine-swinging with Cheetah
into the rivers of Africa.

Drums pounded through the jungle
as he shouted "umgawa"
to safaris from England.

"Do not go down to that river!"
My mother warned all three sisters
after fried chicken at the Wiedemann's picnic.

"Martz's Grove has two
perfectly good swimming pools."

My dad didn't help matters with his stories
of how he swung from a vine in Dayton
out, out, up, and into the beautiful river,
how he swam alone

to the Ohio side
and back again.

Percussive roars and thumps from outboard motors
called us through a canopy of twisted cottonwoods.
There we saw big water where Nile-like barges
glided silently upriver.

Hollywood's notion of the Congo
echoed in our ears.

When they found us, we were knee-deep
in the wake of a passing speed boat.
"Simba, umgawa!" we yelled to the water skier
tethered behind. She waved and laughed.

Brown water streamlets
slicked our heads.

John Donne and God

I wonder about John Donne and God.
When the poet petitioned a hammer for his heart,
was he really looking for a plumber?

Someone to free a clog, liberate a trap,
pound on a pipe to cause movement
in the slick, viscous contents of his soul?

I think of God later, in the union hall
telling the other plumbers about the dank steps
and the secret underbelly of the temple—

the smell of all that sludge not budging
for so long. And if he weren't God,
he might enjoy a joke or two

at the owner's humiliation and decay.
Instead, his journeymen raise a glass
to the sweet suction of an opened drain.

Requiem

> *The prime requisite for humanity is to improve upon our kind.*
> —Robert Webster

We were children who believed
that stars were still within our reach.
Books taught us that greatness
grew from the inside, and nothing
could stop us if we tried.

We were raised at a time
that questioned war
by parents who went to war.
When songs asked, *what is it good for?*
Absolutely nothing was the answer.

We peopled the world with our children.
(Or some of us did.)
Others were haunted
by science lectures predicting
a world over-crowded
with no water, no arable land.

We are threatened now
as *enemies of the people,*
card-playing nurses,
money-grubbing teachers,
left-wing elitists
because we used our
student defense loans
to become the first ones
in our families
to ever go to college.

Back then, the way to beat
a nuclear threat,
the Russians,
and tyranny
was to educate
the working class.

It wasn't called *socialism.*
We called it a chance.

The Webster Sisters Discuss Theology

In a dark blue bedroom
three sisters discuss the nature of God.
Two lie in bunk beds, the oldest sits cross-legged
on what she calls a *Hollywood bed*.
It must be summer, otherwise how are they not
studying math, science, language,
or even the humble pursuit of geography?

Violet likes a white-robed, long-bearded, deep-voiced
Charlton Heston figure
who races over the clouds in a fiery chariot,
his silver hair trailing like a comet,
His will be done above and below.

Rosanne's God favors a friendly uncle
with curly dark hair and bronze skin
who makes lumpy oatmeal to feed her,
pats and smoothes her wispy blonde hair.
accepts and loves her as she is,
without judgment.

The eldest itches to try her theory.
God must be big enough to know
the names of each star, but small enough
to know our names, too.
She nods in the direction of their bedroom window
where the night sky festoons with light.

What if God is the brain of the Universe,
with nerve-endings that stretch
to connect everything that exists?

Violet imagines a brain in a jar.
Like the specimen in Frankenstein's lab,
it contains those crucial bits of glass,
and is labeled "abnormal."
She frowns.
That is the grossest thing I ever heard, she says.

And scary, too! Rosanne adds this with a shiver.
She recalls the *Outer Limits* episode
where a man evolves unchecked
into a mega-brained maniac who views
other humans as lowly, mindless insects
clicking and buzzing their meaningless drones.
She whimpers.

The eldest sighs as she plops down on her pillow to dream
about webs braided with green, purple, and turquoise threads
that spin both galaxies and molecules into whole cloth.

That Kind of Woman

I am the kind of woman who forgets that I am not as tall
as most people. Who once jumped out of her car
to remind the county cop who pulled her over (for nothing)
that this was not a police state yet.

The kind of woman who now wonders who that woman was
and how she felt that strong and how she landed on both feet
in the berm's gravel to square off with that surprised patrolman
on US 27 in the fading daylight of the late 1970s.

I am the kind of woman who believed all my daddy told me:
that I could be a lawyer, a senator, a college graduate—
all those things that eluded him—if I went to school, got all A's,
read good books. Because he didn't know how hard that might be.

I am the kind of woman who wanted to be a priest,
who wanted to be a psychiatrist,
who wanted to be a cop.
Instead, I became a teacher.
Some might say I achieved all my dreams and nightmares.

I am the kind of woman who might chase a bear up a tree,
who sometimes says exactly what the TV will say next,
who walks her sundowner dog up the long driveway at 3 am.

I am the kind of woman who had no children of her own,
but who worries still about what her students were doing
with the other 23 hours of the day she didn't see them.

I am now the kind of woman who won't kill the orb weaver
who plots the web-of-all-webs across my basement door,
hoping for that big catch when I walk through.
While I see the humor in that spider's plan,
I still believe in the passion of craft,
how thread spun in a fever just might hold.

Migration

I sit in the last row at Cindy's funeral—
my childhood friend with whom
I'd swapped stories and comic strips
in the fallow summers between years
at Grant's Lick Consolidated School.

I hear her younger brother give
the eulogy for that bucolic life,
the same one my parents shaped
for me. The uprooting, the packing
into the '53 Chevy, the cheap land

for veterans. "We left Covington to run
those woods," Cindy's brother says. "We thought
we struck gold in the creek. Hell, we knew
we'd hit oil." I see Phillips Creek, the safaris
with my Dad in that dusty rose Jeep. My sisters

turned over rocks for salamanders,
knee deep in the limestone pool.
We left Newport on a Sunday in July,
waved goodbye through Chevy cozy wings
to Buddy, to Pam, to Sylvia.

To streetlights, and stoops, and corner stores.
To row houses packed with factory workers,
to extended families, to narrow strips of concrete yards,
to wagon bridges, to railroad tracks across
the street, to miles of passenger cars as they

howled by each night, shaking our bunkbeds.
Daddy drove west, down 12th Street
to the steamy mirage of Licking Pike.
There he turned south toward a memory
from a story his grandfather whispered.

Elegy for My Ancestry Kit

I wanted to know for sure
Grandma Stephens' maiden name
who answered Great Grandma's
litany when she chanted
"Arthur, Clifford, Frankie"

I wanted to prove stories
about indentured servants
my Grandpa Stephens' first wife
the baby his in-laws would not
let him raise

I wanted to color in those spaces
left between Scotland and County Cork,
figure out why Grandpa Webster joked
about painting our asses green
at the court house

I wanted to dig up linguistic roots
for "waspers" and "it-it"
(from Grandma Babe's mouth
to God's ear) plant a cedar
climb muted branches

I wanted so much to sing their music
at last—my people
those tribes in Montana
those farmers in Meigs and Estill Counties
those railroad families who followed tracks
from Virginia to English to 12th Street
those immigrants from Germany, Scotland
and Russia by way of Ireland or not

All I have to do
is spit in a tube
and mail back
one tiny box

My chest thumps polyrhythms
like a drum near the edge of camp fire
where I cup one ear to the night wind
and ask a pie-shaped graph
to chart our wayward songs

Rosaries

I can't read faces,

you remind yourself
while soldiering through the setlist
at the first assisted living
for the day.

The smiling 90-something twins
in matching fire engine red sweaters
and lipstick seem to cheer you on
with painted grins, yet you hear one bellow:

*Is that a dress she's wearing
or some kind of long blouse?*

It's 95 degrees in the Kansas shade,
so you chose to wear your favorite
too-long-for-a-tunic Goodwill dress
bare-legged with cowboy boots.

*Why does she keep laughing?
I can't hear a thing she says.*

One of the twins clatters off
for the dining tables
where she drags her sister
by a matching red sleeve.

They can't really hear.

This comment comes
from one of three women
seated on the couch.

She offers these tender words
with a long-practiced grace
for brushing crumbs from the corner
of a child's mouth.

I figured as much.
You answer as you launch
into your folksinger's schtick
about required sing alongs.

To your surprise, their voices swell
into all verses and choruses
of "You are My Sunshine,"
mimic expertly your own tune's echo line:
"I'm singing this happy song."

Harmony weaves from the back row
where a tiny woman frowns
Then, a third part chimes
from the couch as another woman leans forward,
her hair tilted in up-do.

Posture and expression inscrutable,
she approaches as you pack your guitar,
shakes your hand. Her face folds into smile:

I used to play accordion
with my mama in church.
She played guitar.
I love singing like this.

The frowner from the back of the room
crowds in to apologize for the lipstick twins.

I get so frustrated at them!
What's your name? she asks.

She etches your name carefully in black ink
on her narrow memo pad.

You are name eight hundred and four.

She offers you a pink crocheted heart
that trails a long tassel.

I pray for everyone on this list.

You imagine her bowing each morning
to strange names, braiding bright yarn
under breath of prayers.

Touchstone

After sweat lodge, MJ explains bear medicine
to the circle of women gathered at retreat.
Drums pound Ojibwa songs about feathers dancing,
Na-na, Ne-na. "Give each other something you hold dear," she says.

I pass my Turkish necklace to the woman just left of my elbow
who cradles a crusty rock criss-crossed with petroglyphs.
Novenas rush to my lips in offering for the rope of beads
I release: ornament, yet rosary.

Give-away loosens one noose of attachment.
New prayers rub sandstone litanies against my fingertips.
MJ burns tobacco and sage for the elk hide drums,
whispers, "spirit beings" while we chant in vocables.

"Always wrap your drum in a blanket," she advises.
I press cool blessings into callouses that no longer yearn,
close wounds in my chest with healing steam
that rises from my throat in ululations.

Song
      (After "Gift" by Judith Hemschemeyer)

Let me tie this song around your finger--
Not now--when the bold print of your life,
like a high definition billboard
is reminding, prompting you along,
hosts of bright exits announcing every turn.

But later, if ever you follow a dark ramp into the loop,
and signs blur, or mumble "no-re-entry" or stop your breath
with the jolt of "dead end."
Then unwind this twine to find the tune again,
a spare thread for your journey home.

The Bear Medicine

I had to have that bear hat.
There we were among the high contrast
black and white photographs of Ansel Adams,
but that's what I bought.

Our Danish neighbors at the first campsite
spent all day scaling El Capitan,
then all night draining gallon jugs
of wine from the camp store.

We crawled out of our tent next morning
to a ten-foot high pyramid of empty bottles
that glittered with impressive precision
in the first slants of Yosemite Valley sun.

At Mariposa Grove where big sequoias grow,
we camped next evening near the river,
opened our own California stash
from the day's vineyard tour.

After the second bottle, I placed the bear hat
on my head—two sets of eyes and ears,
two noses, but just one mouth slurred
in conversation with Gary.

We talked about the rogue bear that rampaged
through the campsite earlier that day.
"Do not leave your food in the tent,"
the ranger had warned us.

"A bear will come to your campsite.
Do not leave your food outside
your car in your cooler.
A bear will come to your campsite."

"Where's that bear?" I boasted so bravely
in my bear hat. "I'll teach that bear a thing or two."
Gary snorted each time I asked the question.
So, of course, I kept asking, "where's that bear?"

Just as we decided to roll into the tent,
the mob scene from every *Frankenstein* movie
played out before our blurry eyes:
Twenty campers chased a young bear

down the river toward us.
As they shouted and waved their lanterns,
his shadow hulked and snarled at them
before splashing into the shallow river.

The torch wielders retreated in mumbles
that rumbled and echoed back to their fire rings.
After that, we couldn't sleep. We sat by the embers
of our campfire to listen for huffs or splashes.

Soon, wine and warmth worked their spells.
Just when the glow of coals lured me
into upright snooze, we heard the bear
in the water as he rummaged

through our sleeping neighbors' cooler
which they—in their city folk wisdom—had tied
in the current for some free refrigeration.
"Oh, no you don't!" I jumped up and grabbed the Coleman

from the young bear's claws.
His mouth flew open at this strange challenger—
half bear, half human—and let out a squeal
like my cat does when I fling her off the kitchen table.

Up the big tree he went
with a bag of French fries,
leaving me with the cooler
which I safely locked in the car.

He crouched on that high branch
for a half hour to pelt us with frozen spuds.
Finally he slid down the opposite side of the trunk
to lumber down the campsite path.

Fires blinked in his shadow like a string of Christmas lights.
Gary shuddered at the wind off the river.
Only then did we realize we would have to sleep
in a tent by a tree that a bear just climbed.

What's Missing

In my poems, the monks
don't set themselves on fire
like they did in Saigon.

They chant low growls
that drown screams of sacrifice,
chime out grief with singing bowls.

They embrace all smoke as incense,
all blood, maroon mantles of procession,
all flame, orange flutter of robes.

I write these words for you
there on the sidewalk.
Your camera shakes

like a creature who quivers
in tall grass, lone witness
over snapping twigs.

You and I practice rhythms
to keep from flying apart.
We rock from side to side,

autistic groundhogs caught
between summer's last tomato
and the barren dark of a quiet burrow.

In my poems, the monks
never set themselves on fire,
but maybe they should.

Roberta Schultz plays guitar, sings and writes for the Kentucky women's trio, Raison D'Etre, who have 9 recordings and one live concert DVD to their credit. They are adjudicated to Kentucky's Performing Arts Directory since 2000. Her song lyrics "January Thaw" and "The Papers" are published in two *Motif* (Motes Books) anthologies edited by poet, Marianne Worthington. While two of her songs made it to the second round of judging in the Great American Songwriting Contest, "Sure Thing" was a 2013 finalist. Her song, "Broken Radio," was awarded Judge's Choice in the Mountain Valley Arts Songwriting Competition, judged by Pierce Pettis.

After attending the SoLaTiDo Song-writing Retreat in North Carolina for many years, Schultz completed her first solo album of original songs, *One Small Step*, with Richard Putnam of Big Feat Productions on key-boards, accompanying and arranging.

She is the author of two previous chapbooks of poetry published by Finishing Line Press, *Outposts on the Border of Longing*, 2014 and *Songs from the Shaper's Harp*, 2017.

Schultz was a regular contributor of book reviews to *Around Cincinnati*, a culture and arts program that aired for the past 15 years each Sunday on NPR affiliate, WVXU, produced by longtime Cincinnati jazz and blues host, Lee Hay. She also worked as an Arts in Healing musician and drum facilitator for Cincinnati Arts Association.

www.ingramcontent.com/pod-product-compliance
Lightning Source LLC
LaVergne TN
LVHW041558070426
835507LV00011B/1171